I0489075

How To Sell Consulting Service?

Essentials On Consulting Business Start Up

Volodymyr Horak

Table of Contents

Description

As I write this book I try to imagine you, those who reads the text on the screen of his laptop or smartphone. I try to understand what are your motives to buy this book, because I'm a business consultant myself and the owner of the company "Training and Consulting."

I will try to answer on important questions for you. I expect that my answers will be so precise that you might want to recommend it to your friends.

I have over 10 years of advice in the optimization of business processes, sales and client-orientation of business. Each of you have your own methods of counseling, which is formed from previous experiences. Hence, I will not give you an advice on how to consult clients with your specialty. Such is not so important for success in consulting. You may even successfully choose an optimal method of consulting by yourself. Do note though

Therefore, I will not give you advice on specialty on how to consult clients because it`s not so important for success in consulting. You might successfully choose an optimal method of consulting by yourself. At the beginning of your own consulting business you will encounter an important challenge: how to build a system of communication with the client.

In this book, I'll concentrate on those questions that troubled me and my colleagues in 2005 at the beginning of my consulting business. Many of the answers had searched intuitively, analyzing their own mistakes, seeking the right decisions.

In this book, I'll concentrate on the answers to the following questions:

- How to move from the role of an employee to a business consultant. What are the issues you need to consider to help you make decisions? I will give you some valuable tips;

- Try to just choose the right strategy and decide on necessary set of services in your business. Your success in consulting will depend on that. Most likely in 2-3 years you will change strategy but you have to start with something;

- How quickly you get customers in consulting business if for your no one knows. I will share two practical approaches;

- What should be the effective scheme with the future client. Stepping scenario arrangements for consulting with the customer;

- Consulting is a business, not just self-employment. Help with guidelines which should seek in the consulting business. I'll tell you what the circuit scale consulting business.

Consulting Beginning. What is Needed for Future Business Consultant?

To engage in consulting practice independently and not in the state of consulting firm, you must understand what you will need.

- Specialized degree in area which you will consult in the future. Itself education does not gives you skills, only knowledge and horizons. But this is the ground on which you may build a foundation of skills and experience.

- Practical experience and accurate results. What experience can be considered sufficient? A reference point for you can be a period of 3-5 years. It is time you start a good understanding of system operations, which guarantees result. Particularly valuable is an experience working with an experienced, mature professional manager (director).

- Method. This is really important. Methodology – sequence of analysis on problems, solving problems. Each method has its own special techniques, skills and tools you'll solve the problems of the customer;

- Strategy of consulting services and creating a consulting business. Understanding of own professionalism. Clear understanding for someone who, in what sequence you will provide consulting services;

Maybe it will not be news to you, and you realize that you do not necessarily immediately begin a career in the consulting business as your own business. You can use the transition period that will allow you to understand if consulting really your thing.

Start in Consulting With no Risk

Internal consultant for the company. Starting a consulting business has significant advantages:

- Regardless of your position in the company, you understand business and its problems;

- The likelihood of you getting a new position since you will be participating in the project, expectation of you working on it;

- You have financial stability. You get paid;

- Within your office, you can avoid errors. But remember not to make the same mistakes repeatedly;

- You have no formal barrier in communicating with managers in the company.

Develop a proposal for a new project in the company, which is being worked on. At the same time get the experience of selling the benefits of the project. Whatever is not concerned, take the initiative.

Being an innovator in familiar team is quite easy. However, your priority is to improve its own method of consultation and the implementation of changes, not to achieve recognition.

Individual consulting services for managers of third parties without creating a separate company.

Starting consulting by one time consultation also has its benefits:

- You have a time to build a circle of acquaintances;

- Each of your project you can be done very carefully, completely focusing on results;

- You'll appreciate how much time you need to implement specific consulting solutions;

- Giving occasional advice, you understand some peculiarities of negotiations with the customer;

- You will be able to hone every detail of consulting methods from completing the questionnaire client to the software that you will use for the preparation of reports;

- Individual consults give you a time to form a circle of prospective clients. Getting to know on exhibitions, conferences, business clubs with new people, share business cards, specifies not only own position but professionalism in consulting.

For example, I specialize in the field of a quick withdrawal of new products to the market, and now I`m working as a marketer in "N". So you gradually build up a reputation as an expert and get the first order. In addition, you will be offered payment for successfully implemented consultation. Invest or save the money.

   They will need you in the future for active development consulting business.

Consultant in social or state project. Check the open positions or offer your services to public organizations, state funds their expertise. Most likely you will be offered low-paid work, but the experience of these projects will form the basis of your portfolio.

The work in the social and public projects are also advantageous:

- You can work with people, values and business experience are significantly different from your;

- You will get invaluable experience to explain complex ideas in simple language without complex terms;

- Public and social funds easier to give positive recommendations and reviews are deployed;

Business consultant as a head and the main expert in his business.

When you decide to make consulting as your main source of income, at once you will get the status of the entrepreneur with all the opportunities and risks of entrepreneurship.

While it is true that there are benefits more than of being a disadvantage to owning a business, do not forgetthat you are not only responsible for the projects of customers, but also for yourself and your family.

- The development strategy of the business. The main indicator effectiveness - contracts with customers for a long 3-6month period of consultation and consulting;

- Systematic financial income. The main performance indicator - the opportunity to share cash flow to provide two separate budgets. The first - the budget for development consulting business, the second - the family budget. It is important that once the funds properly distributed;

- Timely payment of taxes. Keep all of your agreement, receipt of payment is in order;

- Fame and reputation of your name and company. The main performance indicator - a schedule of invitations to business conferences, meetings, treatment recommendations for new customers;

Work in consulting company. And of course, one of the obvious ways to enter the consulting business - consultant work in one system consulting companies or offices.

Statements generally own opinion on such a start from my experience in several projects with consultants of large consulting companies. After working for 4-5 years as a consultant, you get to experience performing complex tasks but primitive.

You do not possess the skill to see the whole situation in the business system. In addition, loading multiple projects at the same time greatly reduces the quality of the results.

Although there are advantages of such a start in consulting:

- The ability to get concentrated experience in projects with experienced colleagues

- The good reputation of a well-known consulting company will add weight in their business negotiations

- Stable payment

To survive and be successful in the consulting business choose your strategy and carefully select the services you'll provide.

This is, and how to scale consulting business, I will discuss below.

How Much a Business Consultant Can Earn?

I'll give you examples on salaries of business consultants. These are examples of salaries offered by domestic consultants. Private consultants can earn 40-50% and at a reasonable scaling, 150-200% more. But the costs Of doing consulting by yourself canbe more.

Salary Survey in United States in Business Consultant

The salary figures below are monthly salaries. You can switch to yearly figures Switch to yearly salaries

Average Monthly Salary in United States in Business Consultant: 6,216 USD

Other Reports: Job Satisfaction Survey   General Job Statistics

Average and Median Monthly Salary Comparison in United States in Business Consultant

Maximum: 13,750 USD

Average: 6,216 USD

Median: 5,833 USD

Minimum: 1,800 USD

Business Consultant VS Business Planning VS All Jobs

Average Salary in United States in Business Consultant	6,216 USD
Average Salary in United States in Business Planning	7,341 USD
Average Salary in United States (all jobs)	6,036 USD

Average Monthly Salary in United States in Business Analyst: 6,882 USD

Other Reports: Job Satisfaction Survey   General Job Statistics

Average and Median Monthly Salary Comparison in United States in Business Analyst

Maximum: 10,417 USD	
Median: 7,333 USD	
Average: 6,882 USD	
Minimum: 1,223 USD	

Business Analyst VS Business Planning VS All Jobs

Average Salary in United States in Business Analyst	6,882 USD
Average Salary in United States in Business Planning	7,341 USD
Average Salary in United States (all jobs)	6,036 USD

Salary Comparison By Job Title (Average Monthly Salary)

Some jobs pay more than others. Displayed below is the salary comparison by job title. Clicking on any of them will display data only for the chosen item.

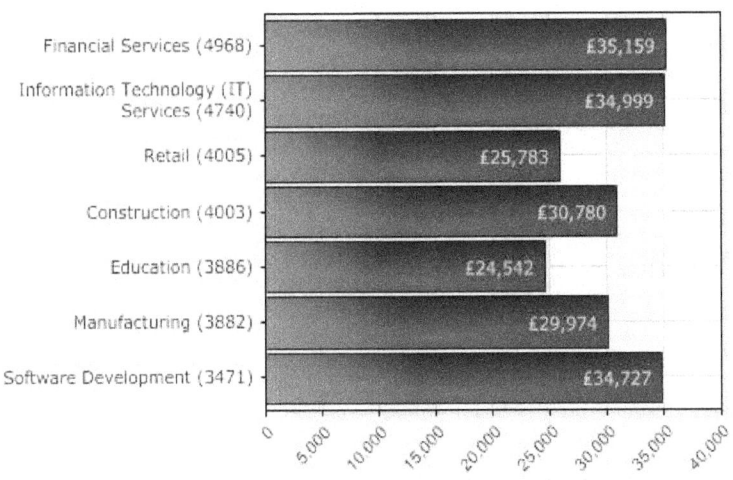

Financial Services (4968)	£35,159
Information Technology (IT) Services (4740)	£34,999
Retail (4005)	£25,783
Construction (4003)	£30,780
Education (3886)	£24,542
Manufacturing (3882)	£29,974
Software Development (3471)	£34,727

Currency: GBP | Updated: 28 Mar 2016 | Individuals Reporting: 169,466

The ability to make money is not the last question of making a decision to do consulting. However, Pareto 20/80 rule applies in consulting business. I think you understand that in order to get 20% of the highest paid consultants, act unconventionally.

A variant of unconventional solutions can be:

- Start consulting business in the region with a small (or very low) professional competition;

- Focus on the domestic corporate market. Creation of a consulting company for the group of companies consisting of great concern;

- Creation of a consulting company in the specific niche in which very few experts but extremely rapid economic growth;

High earnings are important, but for some may not be a motive to start.

 Indeed, if your driving motive is of independence, the ability to choose projects for work, the expert own reputation, high level of your surroundings фis enough to think about own consulting business.

6 Factors That Make a Profitable Consulting Business

In the first month, you need to check six important ideas. A checking, decide to implement them.

1. What do you suggest?

May be a funny questions, but this is a question you will hear 100% from the potential customer. Try to give your child even clear answer what is the result of your advice. What will change for the customer after your cooperation?

Do not describe how you achieve this. What results. Play the game "Convince yourself". Record 20 statements on why you should not be the case and each of them reasonably deny. Your diplomas, certificates, your achievements at work, unique methods, results and feedback your customers use when reasoning.

Until you have come up with very obvious reasons to order consulting services, it is better not to start negotiations with potential customers;

2. Are you able to sell your services? First 6-12 months, most likely you will meet themselves with customers and sell their services. Unfortunately, for orders, simple explanation that you know how to write software or business plan will not be enough.

We'll have to learn to speak in a special way. Ask to answer the question. For example: "What do you specialize? - Do you or your partner had problems with loans at raising funds to expand their business to other countries?" If the answer is "Yes, there" - you briefly explain that this is due to the lack of financial justification payments, due to the ignorance of the tax laws of the country of the importer. And this you specialty. If the answer is "No" - you short say that the circle of your interests associated with the foreign tax expert.

It should develop the ability to find and articulate the key customer problems. You need to sell expensive, so the problems that you plan to solve or need to be very large or quite painful. Selling your services, you will hear failure and indifference. Get used to getting 200-250 proposals, 2-3 meeting invitations. A meeting of 10-15 5-6 orders for a beginner, is good.

Now count how much is the monthly cost of your services for you to efficiently perform 5 orders, while you have operating costs and the need to pay taxes.

3. Do you have enough savings to last financial period for the first several months of serious projects?

The period from casual to permanent contracts and for annual projects can be called "dark zone". Pass it relying on a mathematical calculation impossible.

No model study market potential does not answer the question: "How much will my customer?". Only believing in their success and plucking patience and doing the right steps described in this book, it is possible to do.

So answer the important question as you need funds to survive this period. This may be 4-5 and 10-12 months.

4. What resources do you have?

To bring all resources, is allowing you to generate orders and money. Free room, your laptop, the software license written by your wife (or husband) who can stay with the kids, your acquaintances, old friends and their acquaintances, teachers, your former employers, free internet.

Write down in a separate table of resources.

The first column - material and intellectual resources that allows you to generate solutions consulting.

The second column - dating and relationships that allow you to save money, avoid unnecessary costs or get acquainted with potential clients.

Everything you currently have and that allows you to earn without investing additional funds - your resources.

I started in the first 3 months of calls to potential customers on their way to an internet club, and there held the first consultation through Skype. You do not need an office, expensive furniture, expensive laptop, and business clothes when starting up.

5. How long will you work

Only respond "as necessary." Otherwise, it will not be business and will not work, as a result you will burn professional for the first year.

Determine what will work for 10-11 hours a day in 6 days. Take the rest of the other important areas of their lives.

Otherwise, your health, your relationships with family and frien ds will be greatly affected. Count objectively the time for each project. Most of the time does not take on the project and the way to customer expectations meetings, revision and modification project details, telephone calls.

6. Consulting for you is this job or business?

If the first month you choose your scaling strategy consulting services, will remain forever in consulting well-paid performer. And it gives satisfaction, no significant profits. Scale Consulting projects in several ways. This I will discuss a little further.

Consulting. Who is Offering?

Consulting a search, addressing topical and complex customer business problems using authoring methodology artist, his skills, with a high guarantee of a positive result.

Visit the following link to understand the basic services offered by the Market Consulting. You will learn the most famous offering 30 consulting companies reference - http://www.vault.com in the «best-consulting-firms-prestige, the addresses of sites of consulting companies. Here's a photo from this site. The first five has not changed for several years. You do not necessarily repeat them in sentences. Use their ideas as a focus for the formulation of their proposals.

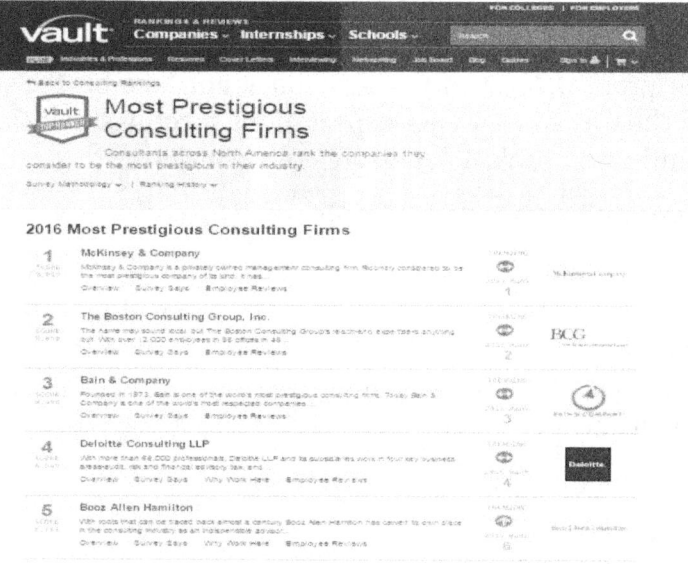

Types of Consulting

Consulting should deal only with those problems that cannot solve semi-skilled workers or solution that must be properly organized by teamwork. When the problem is difficult for the owner of the business, the greater the amount the client is ready to pay for solutions.

Not necessarily your consulting services should be as ambitious as the five leading consulting companies. Indeed, such services as financial audit business, market research, strategic planning, team building communication in large corporations always need.

However, if your service solves an important customer problem, your services will be needed and will be in demand.

For example, services such as programming, evaluation values, the motivation of employees and the development of comprehensive, effective program of motivation for the team or graph diagnostics, recruiting or tax optimization for an entrepreneur is very specialized and thus the desired service.

However, most businesses do not always know how to formulate the reservation and used to take consulting services in areas. To being a dialog with future customers, you better understand what customers expect.

Legal Consulting. This is service is on advising companies on contracts, legal support of company assets, protection of property and intellectual interests of the company.

Financial Consulting. Service on evaluation of assets, assessment of business plans of business units, providing reasonable estimates and recommendations as economic activities, assessment of the accuracy of accounting in the enterprise.

Management Consulting. Assist in the development of enterprise development strategies, assessment, and assistance in the development of regular, relevant and effective management solutions, training manager's management skills. Creating a system of project management, defining the areas of responsibility in the company.

—HR. Complex consulting services in management, motivation, training, coordination of employees. Development programs for managers, production workers, and sales managers. The introduction of the latest techniques of business management.

Marketing Consulting. Helping the company introduce or bring a new product to market, increase extent of sales, re-brand the company;

Consulting in the Management of Retail Complexes. Complex support on the stage of site selection for construction of shopping complex, assess the need for an assortment of policy, work with suppliers to control trade flows within the complex.

Engineering Consulting. Maintenance, installation of equipment at the start of production. Development of business processes, placing and connecting equipment that minimizes the cost of production during the start. Engineering consultant implementing complex technology solutions for production.

IT - Consulting. Development of software to solve customer's business problems. Creating the concept of software solutions, software making the software reliable information from all departments of the company, direct programming, training and adaptation of workers to work with the software.

Career Consulting. Focused on assistance in choosing their own career direction. This type of consulting can take place both within the program and retraining of the company, in order to improve increased personal efficiency on leaders - program aimed at increasing the level of skills of the manager.

Team Coaching. Creating shared values in the team, directing the efforts of workers in active creative search business decisions. Defining values leading employees and an adjustment to the work of the head of this team.

Of course, there are other areas that unite in itself two or more above-mentioned options. Perhaps you offer a consulting service that will integrate the multiple directions. But remember the important rule: "Never confuse consulting and counseling."

Necessary Conditions for Your Successful

Consulting Project

In consulting is always a clearly defined problem task, with the expected result. On your part, you implement clear, proven method of solving problems or achieving goals.

Perhaps it sounds harsh, but it is clear you have to hold the line of responsibility for each measure implemented by you. By this approach, the consultant can always guarantee customer to solve his problem.

1: Understand the capabilities and limitations of their methodology. Do not handle the projects in which your method is not suited.

If you are a business process optimization in management consulting do not try this tool to solve all the problems in the merger;

2: Develop a clear, step by step method of achieving resultsfor a client and you need to work on a strict algorithm to be guidelines for planning and avoid future mutual claims. Decide which credentials of the customer you need, how many times and on what occasion you will meet, what results to expect at each stage of the project;

3: To be able to formulate the problem or do it together with the client. In 50% of clients, stated problem has deeper causes, and your job is to point them and decide. Over time you will form a quality questionnaire to Customer, which will detect system problems over which you want to work;

4: Always arguments specifically agree to project results. Even when appearing on the implementation of additional tasks remember the goal. Your work will be judged by an agreed outcome. Change methods and tools achievement, ask for more money for a job or authority but never fail to allow the parties agreed objectives;

5: Tackle complex projects but those values that you share. You will be hard put maximum effort if you do not share the values of the business customer. For example, if your values are opposite to the values of tobacco or alcohol companies. In practice, the consultant is very important not only to have a high-quality, proven methodology but also harmonize their lives with consulting activities.

To test their personal willingness to enter into this business offer to respond to a questionnaire.

Accordingly, the more "yes"answers, the better is your willingness

1) Your life is well balanced between work and family. At least 70 work for 30 families.

2) Your family supports you in the new activity by 99%

3) Can you sell and you will have time to "hunt" for new customers?

4) Do you have alternative sources of income? At least 2

5) Do you want to build a consulting business, not just change one job to another?

6) You do not deny the hardships of those who cannot afford your services

7) Do you take part in specialized seminars, training and conferences 1 time in 6 months?

8) Do you enjoy and profession specialization, what are you doing

9) Do you exercise, at least 2x a week?

10) You can explain three short sentences of work that resulted with you getting a customer

11) Do you have values in your life are important and you do not yield?

I hope that answers "Yes" you are more "8"

The Principle of Operation of Consulting Business

The consulting business is marketing 2 positions:

- 4 marketing strategies and positioning
- 6 types of services. Have more to consider it

The purpose of the first position potential starts a dialogue with the customer. To form an idea about their potential customer's professionalism idea and sell it as a project. For this, show to the customer how you can easily solve complex problems.

The purpose of the second form is the Extent of business for consultants. At this time form the project of cooperation with the customer. Objectives Project Coordinator correctly formulate the problem and bring it to the desired result;

So when you see promotional offers turnkey solutions for companies on sites promise in the ads, presentations, brochures - you see only the first marketing position. This is the only way in which a company sells its professionalism to his future customers, but not the consulting product. Incidentally, seminars, online channels on YouTube, short training programs all intended to demonstrate professionalism consulting firm or an individual expert.

This option perfectly shows the central page. We see only a facade, areas of cooperation and not the work itself that do suggest consulting company customers.

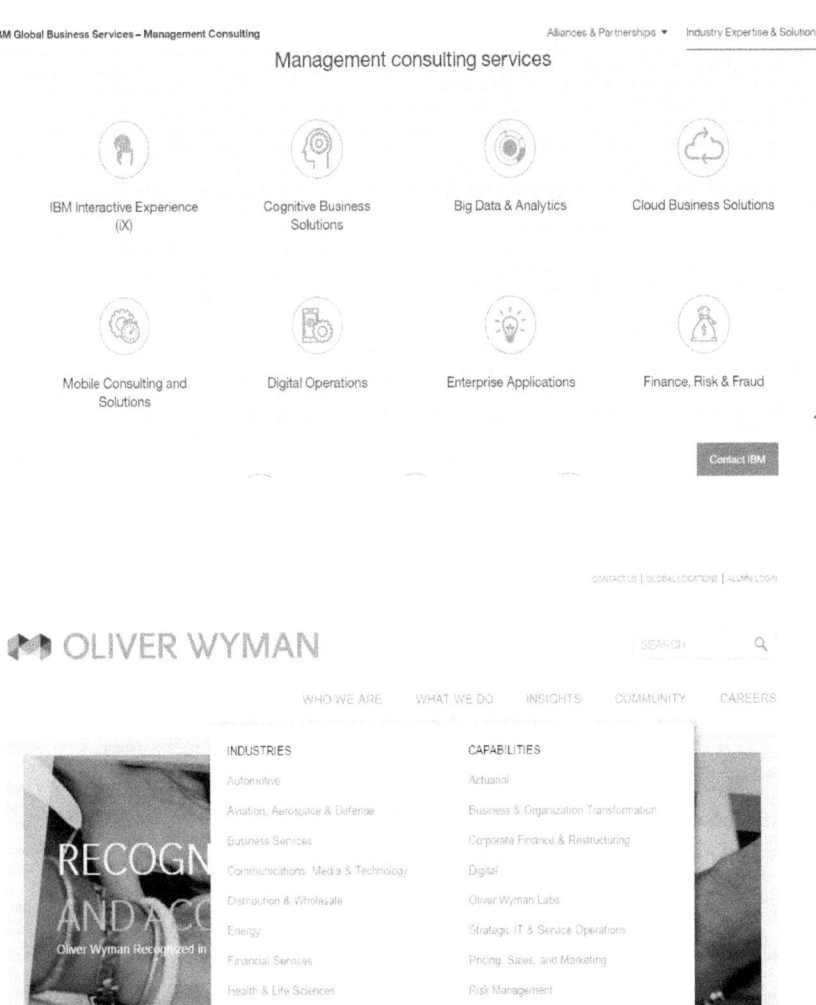

The second item is a marketing consulting business - the formation of the draft decision. Business is done with the future client after greeting for its business problems and presentation solutions.

The other side appears after the initial contact with experts consulting company.

The most difficult in this part is correctly formulateing the problem of the customer. 90% of the time consultant during negotiations on the future design spent on discussion of approaches, methods, areas of responsibility, specific methods which consulting company would solve its task.

At this stage, it will be essential, questionnaires, author tests, diagnostic methods that will clearly identify the real problem with which to work.

Your future reputation, recommendations, and decide regular customers all depend on your performance in this moment.

A key problem is the possibility to include in the draft one or all 6 types of consulting services.

4 positioning strategy consulting business market

The first strategy: - consulting company created to service a large corporation which includes many other businesses. In such strategies dominate: evaluation, audit businesses.

For example, most of the work of audit companies that provide financial, legal, tax audit;

The second strategy: - consulting company is based on the popular business school, practical use, implementing intelligent solutions for the industry market, which is actively developing.

It is found in the IT industry, agribusiness, manufacturing, educational sphere, and trade. In such a strategy dominated by services: perform skilled work, skills training, and sales of research results;

The third strategy: - the company is based on practical experience by new founders. This strategy dominated personal fulfillment sophisticated types of work and transfer the knowledge on workers, the unique customer.

For example, marketing services, alternative sources of energy, rebranding services, services for the adaptability of workers at the confluence of the companies;

The fourth strategy: - sale time highly specialized experts, professionals due to the fact that the market is a regional demand but the lack of qualified personnel.

This strategy dominates partnership, interaction design highly skilled workers;

There is fifth model - to try to come up with the heel model. But you may unlikely like this approach.

Consulting. 6 Types of Professional Services

- Perform skilled work (services). The resulting unique specialist experience in their field whether it is production, recruitment, translation, construction pits, opening shopping centers, development of the site allows the consultant to do the job quickly and efficiently, and save your customer time and money by working with the consultant.

- Assessment (audit), implementation of effective schemes of work through changes in the customer's business. In this approach, the consultant has a certain ideal model of the program but implements it in hands of the workers themselves or a company manager. The role of the consultant in this approachis to direct and coordinate the work.

Another requirement of audit is to help make an accurate "diagnosis" of the client. Expected result - realized based system solve customer problems which may include: training, development of methods of interaction between departments, optimization of each department, changing the system of motivation or business management;

- Training of necessary skills. Direct learning of new, actual technologies for customer, methods, techniquesg the client;

- Sales for the results of their own research methodology. Research develop methodologies and most research results can be replicated, such methods of describing business processes in the company's service standards in the company, motivational climate assessment methodology, causes change of work, key employees, reasons for purchase, and others;

- Mediation. The extent of involvement performance of the customer partners from other industries, qualifications which are very high. The role of the consultant in such projects is a coordinator.

Of course, you cannot have all the skills to optimize the business, for this shape the card with business partners who specialize in subjects related to your approach. For example, if your business is recruiting workers, mediation of business coaches will be very successful;

Now I hope you understand what is the nearest purpose in creating consulting business. Have thoroughly dismantled the entire process of creating an output for the profitability of your company.

Let's summarize something worth considering to decide whether consulting business is worth your time. Give a written response to the 5 theses:

1. You understand your strategy consulting business;

2. You know that 6 kinds of services you can offer to its clients;

3. Do you know what the result of the uniqueness of your product or service and how you will gradually implement its business customer;

4. Do you know what the customer expected professionalism consultant;

5. Do you have suggestions variants of cooperation after the first client card with you;

The Right Start in the Consulting Business

I deliberately do not use the term "fast start" because, in this case, the accuracy is more important than speed. What I recommend you is you check my practice and my consultant colleagues.

So, without which, you cannot do it at the beginning - environment for selling their services.

If you are currently a working employee, the most important task that you need to decide is:

- Select a place for the sale of which will require consulting services

- To form the environment in which you will be taken as expert and business consultant;

- Create your new friend's willingness to share with you of their problems in business;

- Develop confidence in your advice, an advisor who can guarantee the promised results;

To solve these problems, you should immediately concentrate on four areas of work:

- Promoting yourself as consultant

- Investments in instruments of communication with potential customers

- Rational organization of the process of project implementation

- Development of new offers for existing customers

I propose to consider each of these areas in more detail.

Perhaps unpleasant news to you will be that the promotion of their services first 2-3 years will have to deal with you personally. No advertising or managers will not do what is your objective, "Develop a reputation of being an efficient business consultant."

Write articles, shoot video, write books, reports, reviews, act, give interviews - it becomes your usual work directly beside consulting and business consulting. But there is other not very good news. The quality of your services to the growing number of new projects will average. In other words, the more you will have new customers, the less time you will have to bring to the ideal of every new project.

Implement projects quickly, very efficiently the first time, and always in clear-cut terms. Avoid rework project, quickly implement amendments in the course of its implementation. But remember that every significant additions and enhancements problem is a new project that has a run time and budget. The good news is that it will appear regular customers are willing to pay for such an approach is clear, fast, expensive, and with a guarantee.

- Promoting itself as consultant

To find out about you as a quality consultant, you do not need to immediately invest in expensive brochures, folders, advertising and other trash. Instead "set a gentleman" business consultant need. Cards with contacts on the back of which 3-4 will be your key services, one side have the address of your site on the Internet describing the service results, review your clients (or employers).

And the most important free software solution, for example, you can show how you work. For example, it may be a mini-book or article on "All techniques reduce taxes for entrepreneurs with a turnover of up to 1 million dollars" if you are doing the optimization of income. Or "aggressive recruiting methods unique specialists" if you provide services in recruiting.

- Now to the question of who and where you have to hear to get your application solutions and generally know about your existence.

There are two approaches. The first approach takes more time, but it requires less money.

You should engage in all possible business clubs, public organization dealing with entrepreneurship, support groups, trade shows where you want to hold a free seminar or to exchange contacts with participants, thematic conferences. Do this only when you are formally considered in these groups.

You need to think ways of communicating with members of clubs and organizations. You need to organize their own performances, workshops, short presentations. It is not as problematic as it might seem. You will not necessarily be a brilliant orator. It should be accessible language to talk about what's going on in your program solutions and explain what results can be expected. ThiAll these participants will leave their phone for communication, email address to send the application with other proposals for a thoughtful self-examination. Typically, this approach gives the result after 5-6 months of active work.

So maybe long, but personal card rather reliable source of business communications. It should be noted that it is necessary to take care of matching profile on social networks your image consultant.

What should be a result of this activity:

- List of addresses and telephone numbers of control areas, directors

- Conducted a substantive meeting on future cooperation in company potential customer. Getting to know your business and its problems

- Sent within 2-3 days with detailed commercial offer step by step plan consulting work and decide on the proposal date tentative substantive meeting.

Typically, 20-30 sites, you will be subject to meetings 5-6 and 2-3 order. Do not stop to expand the range of potential customers. To highlight this 3-4 hour per week for the organization, participation, and consultation of events. Only when your working month will be a busy 30 days in advance, you can then think about getting an assistant, who will organize your participation in information events for you.

Techniques explore potential customers may include:

- Writing for a review of the sector. Exchange business cards meet, set highly specialized questions. Write a detailed article with recommendations, everyone who met and get feedback;

- Free independent assessment of the effectiveness of the unit. Offer to work for free and offer the best solutions;

- A proposal to hold a free master class opportunity, to work with your system for 1 hour;

- Statement as potential clients to conduct an independent assessment of the department. Further, draw a mini-report and agree on a meeting with the manager to present your mini-report and further cooperation opportunities;

- Another alternative way to find customers for consulting is a "review of the proposals." Subscribe to vacancies in its focus groups on the sites to find work. Jobs that match your specialization may be a good topic to start a dialogue with potential customers. For most entrepreneurs, announcing a competition for the job with high demands expected a result. And you can guarantee this result. Explain that you can work as a project manager, and the details are ready to discuss the interview. It acts as my colleague, who provides consulting services to build a marketing strategy;

Second intercourse less time but need more money;

In the second approach, you need to find colleagues, clients are not directly intersecting with your consulting services, but the overlap is based on the purchase. For example, if you provide legal services for copyright, it is your closest colleagues or consultants may be company strategic planning, brand company.

Since the owners of these management companies, you agree that you will write a series of articles which demonstrate their approaches to solutions to the problems of clients. And the owners of these consultancies will include them in its weekly newsletter for its customers. Obviously, for this, you need to pay. Try not to use "cold advertising" and interviews, comments urgent customer problems, answers to frequently asked questions. The good news is that if your product consulting is quite expensive, the cost of distribution will be paid on the first order.

Another scheme paid consulting services to promote their writing is stately in thematic magazines. Select required only magazines that do have a high rating and reputation among managers. It is important that the articles in these magazines also have to be very high quality. Therefore, if you have the original level, better use the services of a professional journalist or copywriter.

Such an approach like online advertising is content to apply. However, online competition is very high among consulting and training companies. Therefore, if you start to promote their services online, do it systematically. Start with clear directional quality site design, content, suggestions for its business audience, full of useful materials, references, forms to generate e-mail addresses.

In consulting, it is a very important moment when a potential customer is your customer. This is the time when you are negotiating over the phone or in the office of the customer. As a consultant, you talk about the problems which faced leader in its business. Only this time, you have a chance to get a real order, and not when the customer reads your presentation materials, review your presentation or talk with you about the projects you implemented.

Every article which holds meetings, information materials, advertising that you will send to our partners to explain why it's important to meet and pick up a program of cooperation, would be the best solution for the future of the customer.

Investments in instruments of communication with potential customers

We have to start a conversation with you, and without the presentation itself through a single-site profile in social networks, YouTube channel, it will not be possible.

In this section, we discuss various communication channels and potential clients Functions

Single-site + Blog. Single-purpose your site - and get results demonstrate phone or email leads. Don`t disperse in the names of your website. What site your proposal will be heard? For example: "Online recruiting key employees in 7 days." Website developers certainly offer you appropriate design and explain how your site will implement the e-mail marketing. Look at a typical example of single-site business consultant Ichak Adizes.

Dr. Ichak Adizes — Personal Web Site
Home   Blog   YouTube   Twitter   Pictures   Publishing   Contact

Dr. Ichak K. Adizes, Ph. D.

Over the course of more than 40 years, Dr. Ichak Kalderon Adizes has developed and refined a proprietary methodology that bears his name. The Adizes Methodology enables corporations

E-mail newsletter. Or e-mail marketing, is a way by which you form from the customer loyalty to himself as an expert. Prepare high-quality, valuable information material for the customer in the form of articles, mini-books or videos. Send this story to a prospect in exchange for their email address. Put task developers to customize your site to generate e-mail addresses.

Profile in LinkedIn. Complete your profile details. Add a job, achievement in every place of work, professional skills which are mastered, specialized training which took part, your consulting offer. Be sure at least 1 time per week to post short articles 1200-1500 marks reviews on your specialization. Benefits of LinkedIn is that you can own and actively, through the "advanced search", find CEOs. But do it right. At first, fill your profile with interesting informative materials. Then send your invitation to be added to the business community. From time to time, not more than 1 time per month, ask your business partners to evaluate materials, skills and your professional skills. Immediately place the target of the most active business partners in LinkedIn meet in person.

Profile on Facebook. Facebook is not directly accessible as LinkedIn to form business contacts. The main business activity in Facebook is a specialized group. Join a professional group of 20-50 where your skills can be applied. Try to properly comment, give tips, interesting for the audience to send information, links to seminars and conferences where you will speak with a link to your site or article placed in LinkedIn. It is important to demonstrate a systematic activity to shape its own reputation as an expert in your field. Carefully review their posts on Facebook. Remove all ambiguous and too personal posts. Remember that now the majority of business partners examine new friends just after viewing their profiles on social networks.

Profile on Twitter. This tool has a clear goal - to briefly inform that you are currently taking place. Recommended to actively use this tool when working on multiple projects. When you have "insights" developing, interesting visualization or a team - this place short positions. Give your audience something really impressive. Otherwise, you will be boring to read. Summary in a specialist. We have to think about the need to contact employers seeking professionals your level. To facilitate contact, post a resume extended to all sites and job search month to be renewed. Extended resume - a resume with a cover letter in which you accentuate that you are interested in the project work. Explain the skills that you own, the results of companies with whom you worked, position feedback of their satisfied customers.

Rationally Organize the Process of Project

Implementation

For each project, start a separate profile. Be realistic. Do not handle the projects that do not motivate you or do not have any monetary reward.

Each consulting project is divided into 4 stages:

1. Communication with the client and team

2. Preparation of documents, development of solutions for the customer

3. Verification and testing developments in practice

4. Introduction and adaptation changes

Broken down in 4 steps, it allows you to combine work on multiple tasks customers in a single 3-4-hour session. Simply combine the same type of work in one duty cycle where you make more than your first completed project and then to start a new one.

For example, if you are looking through resumes for recruiting - search resumes for all its customers which will be recruiting unit. At first glance it is obvious, but in reality not all consultants act in this way.

Work in short sessions of 2-3 hours.

Coming up with a reward at the end of each session. This could be cup of cocoa in Chess Party series favorite series, a walk in the park for 20-30 minutes and hundreds of other possibilities to switch and give yourself a short holiday.

Finish projects on time, or just agree on a prolongation of the project. Avoid situations of unfinished project as it will distract you from full concentration on existing projects.

Delegate mechanical work. If you want to make a presentation; type text; prepare invoices; prepare to pay to file; organize seminar; book a hotel; or create, print training materials,delegate an assistant.

In working on the project, completely disconnect all social networks, put mobile phone on silent mode.

Most likely you will have to navigate between the cities and get to meetings on time. If you have little travelling experience, be sure to inquire of faster transportation, or easier way to get into the city within a radius of 100-200 km. Define the schedule, cost, mode of transportation, travel time, the cost of taxis in urban areas, as your alternative.

- Development of new offers for existing customers

First, focus on attracting new customers in 3-4-month project, which will hold the next 2-3 months. After the first half, when you have 18-20 content customers who ordered your different types of services, concentrate in developing new customers for existing consulting offerings. This program can be designed for one month of training. Several workshops are united by a common theme, online training (webinars), together with other consultants' program, or other services that are relevant in this company.

The optimum ratio of concentration attention and development proposals between the new and existing customers should be 30/70. 30% is your free time to concentrate on projects finding new customers and negotiations. While the 70% is on focusing on developing new offers for existing customers.

During the first year you will realize that the constant consulting work with existing customers is pushing you to the idea of scaling consulting business. Think about how other consultants recommend and coordinate the implementation of their projects.

Your Work Plan for the First 6 Months

- Create an offer of collaboration benefitting the client (work, time, result guarantees)

- Think about how you will receive money (a form of work activity)

- Make a one-page site LP with 1-2 and 3 proposal of formats. The best format would be text + video reviews of your clients (or employers), their photos and your contacts. First, this is enough. After 6-7 months, when you really understand what customers expect from you, redesign your website.

Start your Cognitive Journey

Data, in all forms, is expanding as a resource to be utilized. Yet in many industries and professions, the data explosion is outstripping the human capacity to understand the meaning hidden within that data. Cognitive computing is able to unlock the potential in all data - internal, external, structured, unstructured, voice, and visual - and make it work together. Enterprises can make better operational decisions, understand customer wants and needs, communicate in real time, and optimize business processes – infused with the cognitive ability to understand, reason, and learn.

Contact us about a Cognitive Journey workshop to uncover the best areas in your organization to quickly get started with cognitive.

Request a Workshop

Contact IBM

- Develop a series of free e-mail newsletters to potential customers; remove and place on their YouTube videos; write a mini-book with recommendations for future customers.

- Put it all on Landing Page.

DON'T MISS A THING
FREE UPDATES BY EMAIL

Enter your email address

me@email.com

subscribe

or decision making.

Now what?

You can use that surplus to play video games and hang out.

Or you can use that surplus to go learn how to do something that can't be done by someone merely because she has a calculator.

Either way, your career as a long-divisionator was over.

Entire professions and industries are disrupted by the free work and shortcuts that are produced by the connection economy, by access to information, by robots. Significant parts of your job are almost certainly among them.

Now that we can get what you used to do really quickly and cheaply from someone else, you can either insist that you still get to do that for us at the same fee you used to charge, or you can move up the ladder and do something we can't do without you.

Posted by Seth Godin on May 31, 2016 | Permalink

170

- Over 2 months, participate as a speaker in all possible local and regional business environments (organizer, lecturer, Networking Meeting), consider joint activities with consultants and companies that run longer than you.

Find local analogue www.allconferences.com/Business/ sites and take part in all important thematic events.

Global Conference Directory
& Event Planning Solutions

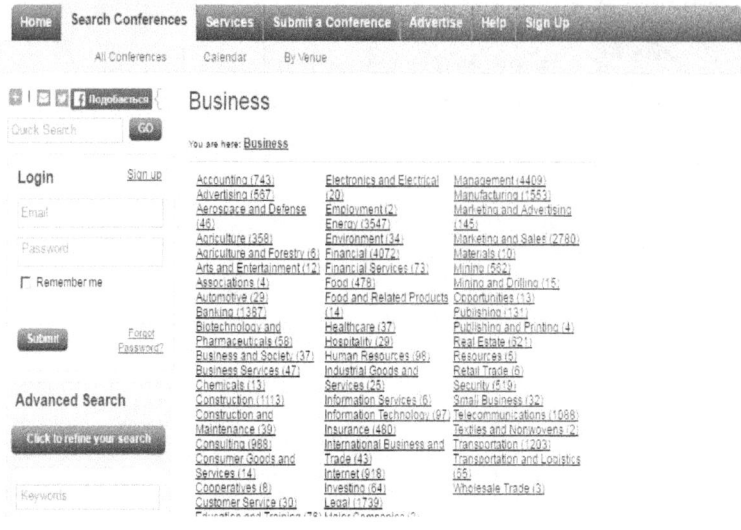

- Adjust your profile on social networks and use social network LinkedIn, Twitter to create your reputation expert.

- Do reviews, create content in their subject;

- Write down a list of all your colleagues who are likely to have the opportunity to organize a meeting with the heads of companies.

Increase Your Consulting Business

Zoom in business - is to find a way to increase sales to customers without significant loss of quality. If you do not find a way to scale its advisory services, consulting remains selling your time for more money, but not business.

Options for scaling:

Partners Consulting. Collaboration with partners who are at the same high level as you provide consulting services. In such, cooperation is important to develop the skill project coordinator. Monitor the timely implementation of obligations partners, service quality, and organize their communications with customers;

Long-term projects. These are orders which could last from 6 months to 1 year and use you for a few hours during the week. Ongoing projects allow you to get higher financial income and build communication channels with new clients or develop new better offers. Long-term consulting projects also enable partners to engage consultants to check their quality work.

Part of the profits from the business customer. This form of agreement with the client includes income you receive when reaching customer company planned financial performance. This works well in those types of consulting services as software development; marketing support company; financial consulting; legal support of purchase and sale of assets;

Own business. Help and advice to other companies you can touch up on the idea of a business. Deeply studying its customer business, sometimes comes to the understanding that the biggest limitation is the founder of the company. That is the idea of creating their own company.

However, I want to warn you to expect the greatest difficulties when zooming consulting business through entrepreneurship.

The biggest difficulty is - you. You, because of how your brain thinks ergo your way of thinking, experience and habitual nature of the work focused on consulting. Specific activities are a bit different in Entrepreneurship.

In consulting, we minimize business risks; while in entrepreneurship, we must be able to live in a constant state of risk. Choose a time when you are ready to live.

Author's school. If your technique is effective, it can open an authoring program training. You can actually submit their technique to professionals who will use it in their business.

Payment Business Consultant

Most business consultants are not fully aware on how they should get paid for advice in business. Some of them are paid hourly; someone is paying for the result; and some asked to be paid

for their work on daily rate. Usually this is because not every advisor understands how to build correctly.

Hourly pay. The agreement is only possible when you have a clear product at the end of the execution time. However, it is not suitable for training, and long-term projects in which you share with participants finding common solutions. This though is a good option for a small permanent income, while a bad approach for a strong start in consulting.

Payment for projects. A very successful form of payment, is conveniently calculated. Project should be very carefully described. The amount of payment depends on your expenses, so maximize the number of projects you can do during the period and the number of calls you do. Pric ae can be determined early on the number of applications, with the growth of your professionalism, indicate the price and take only those projects which give the highest professional and financial returns. Payment for balanced draft payment option for this can be very long (5-8 months) while 1-2 months for short-term or pilot projects.

Payment of part of the profits. This option is ideal if your business is marketing advice, issues purchase and sale of assets of the business. The completed contract has clear financial value, of which you have to pay. This is a good option for high-level experts and stable reputation.

4 Stages of Negotiations With the Customer

Each project has 4 components of success for its implementation:

1 Training program of the project. The program is a major project application to the contract. In the program you must describe in detail: the goal of the project; what do you do; how long you will do the work and place (office, or customer conference room in his office); the result for each block of the project; cost of the project; your powers in the project; and project participants who will be responsible for coordinating the project on the customer side. A separate topic of talks highlights the participation of the leaders of the project. Ask the customer to present your team, explain your powers, objectives, tasks, explain expected final result;

2 Conclusion of cooperation. Ask your colleague lawyer to help you draw up a contract to provide consulting services. You need to think about the way you will pay him. It is important to say it in the contract. The first and second stages are very important for the successful implementation of the project. Pay them enough time. Do not worry, show your professionalism and tackling the "hot work" will be time and opportunity;

3 Final protocols for each important block of the project. End Meetings with the customer are important. At this meeting you will present the results, adjust goals, address or solve current problems encountered at work. Regular meetings, 1 or 2 times a week, will allow you to promptly adjust their work. As a result, you will end your project quickly and without significant changes;

4 The final presentation of the final results of your project. At this point, except presentation, you need to make a proposal to collaborate on these types of services with the justification of the need for each unit.

The final stage can last much longer than the project itself. Qualitative project outcome will generate positive customer feedback about your work. Do not be afraid to get negative reviews. Negative reviews are your benchmarks for success, they will form you as an expert, making greater effort.

Reminder. What you should discuss with the customer:

Immediately agree on clear results that the client expect from you. You need to describe it in the agreement by adding it on the annex of the agreement.

Arrange support from the management company. Since most of the work to be performed by the customer, you need 100% support from his side. Reach agreement on your powers with the company. Get an access to the database, organize and conduct meetings. Clearly explain to the client what kind of results, and in what form and when he can expect it. Give the customer a guarantee of results and to do this, make sure that you understand what is taking responsibility.

Agree on the fee and advance payments. The ideal approach to determining the price is the minimum price at which you are willing to work at the peak of their abilities. Do not Focus on the average market price. Generally, experts have fees ranging from 50-70% higher fee for their work than those of salaried professional employees.

Risks During Arrangements

To begin, conduct and complete a quality project successor and avoid traps that can begin with these phrases:

1. To begin the project, will achieve any results and then see how we will count your fee. Likely they are not going to pay you. Break up the whole project into smaller projects and arrange for the payment made parts. We have a very special situation, so better understand first what is what a few weeks and after people will take you - you will make changes. It is likely that the customer wants to receive a significant

part of consultations for free. Ask the customer to independently formulate what exactly you need to understand take a payment for the findings, diagnosis;

2. I do not know what I need - you are a consultant please advise (or: you will do and I'll see if I fit). The customer waives responsibility for the result and translates it for you. Explain that good cooperation is possible only on partnership terms. If the client does not know what he needs - you will have problems. Give him time to decide. You are not a psychotherapist;

3. People offered me the same service but cheaper. Well, they are haggling with you. Negotiate, explain what they are paying for. Speak phrases which will evident the benefits they could get;

4. Let's do this project by 50%, plan a very active development here and then we will agree on the pay. A typical technique in negotiations - "promising future". Agree that the active development thanks to you, work will come. For this result, they will pay you. Perhaps the reason is not in the price, but in the lack of experience with business consultants;

5. I give you the time and my team, please work. Another way of avoiding responsibility. Always clearly separate powers. Of course, the bulk of the work, you do. You prepare, analyze, implement changes themselves, but most systems solutions, the customer will have to make with you;

Motivational Tips for the Future Business

Consultants

You will want to give up, especially in the first two years, such thoughts will be coming! Give yourself a word that no matter what happens you will stand. Set a clear goal which would be a criterion for success.

For example: "Hold consulting services and get positive reviews 100 most famous companies in the region."

There will be a time when there will be no orders. In general, Survive this temporary calm. Concentrate on improving your technique and develop free informational materials, meet new people. Set a goal for a week - 20 new friends among potential clients and achieve it.

You have to control your finances. It is not always easy, especially in the first 1-2 months. Plan your income and expenses for the month ahead. Remember that each project also has its costs. Consider this when forming prices. Immediately properly allocate for family budget and the budget for the consulting business.

Highlight a permanent part of the family budget out of business. Learn to sell not one counseling, and all six types of services for each client that you will have an order for 6-7 months in advance.

You will have a higher income than now in work for hire. I wish that it was. Invest a substantial part of the money not on these things like a new car, fashion and gadgets.

Rather, invest in lifestyle, quality tools for the job, a new experience, education, environment and knowledge. Strategically it is right. Consulting business is 90% identity and only 10% technique.

Your evenings can be busy working - the first 3 years and weekends too! Work short distances over the weekend.

Divide the needed 4-5 hours on weekends at intervals for 2-2.5 hours with breaks in 3-4 hours that you will spend with the family.

My Conclusions About 10-Year Career as a Business Consultant

It is an incredible feeling to see not the boss, but see your children grow; to taste the most delicious coffee in the morning after successfully completed a six-month project yesterday!

Values of clients are more important than the money they want to pay you.

A romantic story about the dishes of the restaurant can be completed of very boring story of subscribers who you sold advice here. We must to learn to invent new legend of restaurants.

Real interesting people are those who ask wise questions.

It's not important how much you earn in the project,rather, the quality you get and how valuable your new experience will be.

Business consulting may not be the best way to professional fulfillment, but experience in business consulting gives a concentration, which any other job cannot give you!

I am personally wish that you reach the highest peaks in consulting. I hope one day to receive your feedback on how this book helped in your development.

I recommend to read further on the subject:

30 Days to Wealth

The New Code of Money

This book is special. This is a collection of the principles of accumulating wealth and maintaining a successful business. I'm not trying to teach you specific skills. Required skills are formed very quickly.

Let's start with the most important - your subconscious, then formulate the principle of Maximum Abundance for youn within 30 days, from the 90 principles for accumulating wealth. At the end of the month your focus of attention is reliably fixed on wealth.

Everyone who thinks about big money inevitably feel fear. The fear of large-scale goals like becoming a millionaire. No it's not for me, but most say why not? Nowadays in the world there are 14.6 millionaires. Every day it increases by 2.5. Why not be in their ranks?

www.ingramcontent.com/pod-product-compliance
Lightning Source LLC
Chambersburg PA
CBHW061227180526
45170CB00003B/1199